MW00473451

Best Travel Guide to Ireland's Lesser Known Destinations

An itinerary for those who like to venture off the beaten path

K. C. Dermody

Copyright © 2015 by K.C. Dermody

All rights reserved. No part of this publication may be reproduced, distributed or transmitted in any form by any means, including photocopying, recording, or other electronic or mechanical methods without the prior written permission of the author/publisher except in the case of brief quotations embodied in critical reviews and certain other noncommercial uses permitted by copyright law.

Contents

Introduction 5

A Few Tips Before You Go 7

Getting Started: Your First Day in Ireland 11

The Itinerary.. 13

Dublin 15

County Wicklow... 19

County Wexford 25

County Wexford to County Kerry: What to See Along the Way 31

County Kerry 33

Getting to Inisheer Island... 41

Inisheer Island.. 45

County Galway and Connemara.. 51

Ross Castle, County Meath 57

A Final Note 61

K. C. Ðermody

Introduction

Having traveled to Ireland many times, my first book, "Best Travel Guide for First Time Visitors to Ireland," was written to help those travelers make the most out of their trip as well as to make planning their getaway infinitely easier.

My second Ireland-based book is for those who've already experienced that fabulous but well-worn itinerary as well as for those who prefer staying off the beaten path and going to places that are rarely mentioned in most guide books.

As I've extensively covered the basics in my first book, meant for first time travelers to Ireland, such as when to go, what to pack, finding cheap flights, renting a car, exchanging money, etc., in this book, I've included just a summary with a few additional tips I've learned along the way.

This book focuses on a route that will bring you to many wonderful off the beaten path destinations I've thoroughly enjoyed, including some recommended by locals, and castles that aren't typically found in most travel guides.

I don't provide hidden destinations in every county in Ireland as it would take a lifetime to see them all, instead, these are my personal favorites that I was surprised to come upon and believe you'll enjoy too.

This itinerary that will take you from Dublin to the Wicklow Mountains, Hook Head Peninsula, County Kerry and the spectacular southwest, the Aran Islands and, finally, beautiful Connemara, with an optional night in County Meath at an authentic medieval castle, is doable within 10 to 14 days, depending on your travel style, of course, but the more time you have to spend, the better.

I'll provide you with the leads you need to experience a more unique adventure in the Emerald Isle – it's up to you to savor each and every moment.

If you have any questions, I am happy to answer them via comments on my website at www.kcdermodywriter.com, or by email at kcdermody@gmail.com.

A Few Tips Before You Go

Although I included many tips in regard to Ireland trip planning in my first book, there are a few things important enough to go over again, especially considering that when it comes to travel, there are many aspects that can change quickly.

When to go

If you're hoping for the most authentic Ireland adventure, with the chance to really get to know the locals, avoid going in the summer months if at all possible. This is also the most expensive time to go, so you'll reap significant savings when it comes to airfare as well as on accommodations. The downside is that some activities and attractions may be closed in the offseason, but with so much to see and do, this is usually not a big deal, particularly for those looking to venture off the beaten path. By heading to the Emerald Isle in the shoulder season, between mid-September and mid-October or throughout the month of May, you may be able to enjoy the best of both worlds.

Transportation

If you plan to visit a number of destinations, renting a car is the best way to get around. On the other hand, if you're going to spend the majority of your time in one place, you may want to consider train and/or bus transportation which is readily available. Driving in Ireland, as you may already be aware, can be challenging, but the freedom and flexibility are usually well worth the difficulty. After a few days, you'll most likely feel a lot more comfortable.

Do keep in mind that renting a car in Ireland is not like renting a car in the U.S. Comparing prices can be difficult as some include all the charges involved, while others do not. Though you will find familiar U.S. rental agencies in Ireland, they rarely offer the best deal. I've found that Dan Dooley, an Ireland-based car hire company, generally provides the best value. If you have a credit card with a high limit and don't mind having a large amount of money held onto it, Sixt Car Hire may be your best option. If that isn't possible, you'll need to purchase Super CDW, an extra insurance which covers nearly all of your liability if something were to happen to the vehicle. Even if your credit card includes car rental insurance, it will not be accepted in Ireland. Purchasing Super CDW may double the rate you've been given, so be sure you've done your due diligence in checking to see that all fees have been included. You may also want to find out the amount that will be held on your credit card before you get to Dublin to avoid unpleasant surprises.

When selecting your vehicle, avoid mid-sized or larger cars. A compact vehicle with a manual transmission not only saves you money, it offers better control on curves in addition to better handling when negotiating narrow, winding roads. Ideally, secure one that has a trunk that can hold all of your luggage so that it can be stored safely when you're visiting larger cities.

GPS

Investing in a GPS system can make traveling around Ireland infinitely easier, particularly if you're on your own and don't have a travel partner who can read a map as you drive, or vice versa. Most car rental agencies make this an option when renting a vehicle, but it's expensive. If you plan to be there for more than 10 days, it will probably cost as much or even more as buying one. I purchased the TomTom World Traveler Edition for about $160 on Amazon.com and it's been a lifesaver. There are cheaper models available as well. The only downside is that to get directions to certain locations, you need a specific address, and for some more remote sites and attractions, there is no address to enter. The majority of the time, it does the job perfectly.

Exchanging currency

Don't exchange your U.S. dollars to euros at home. Surprisingly, many travelers still think this is the best way to go, but using your debit card at an ATM in Ireland is the least expensive option and the most convenient. Just plan ahead so that you don't incur fees every time you need some cash. You can also use your debit card to purchase items at most establishments just like you do at home. Call your bank to find out if there are foreign usage fees ahead of time first.

Cell phone

Having a cell phone can make traveling throughout the country a lot easier. If you lose your GPS signal or can't locate your Bed and Breakfast, you can easily call and get directions. You'll find that the hosts of many B&Bs and other establishments ask guests to call before to confirm a reservation, so you may need a phone for that too.

Check with your cellular company to find out if your phone will work in Ireland. Many require an international calling plan to be activated. Be sure to inquire about all of the fees that might be incurred, and then just use it on a limited basis. Another option is to purchase a cheap prepaid phone at the airport when you arrive. In fact, it may be less expensive than using your own phone, depending on the rates your current company charges, although it won't come with all the bells and whistles.

As most establishments in Ireland, including pubs and B&Bs, have Wi-Fi these days, people with smartphones, tablets, iPods, and other tech gadgets will be happy to find that it's easy to get internet access just about anywhere you go.

Getting Started:
Your First Day in Ireland

During your first day or two in Ireland, it's best not to plan too much. Flying can be exhausting, and the time difference, eight hours if you're coming from the western U.S., can really do a number on you mentally and physically.

Ideally, don't plan on driving too much. You might want to get a hotel or B&B that's just outside Dublin City Center so that you can walk or take public transportation, exploring some of the city's highlights and hidden treasures. Driving in Dublin is really best avoided at any time, and unnecessary anyway.

Some good options include:

Travelodge Dublin Phoenix Park Hotel with reasonable rates along with clean, comfortable rooms just a short ride on a double-decker bus to the city center.

Deerpark Lodge, a Bed and Breakfast-style accommodation with inexpensive rates, located near the Phoenix Park entrance gates in Castleknock, Dublin, also a short ride to the city center.

Clarion Hotel Dublin Liffey Valley is another value option just west of the city center near Castleknock Castle.

Or, if you'd prefer to avoid going into the city altogether, the town of Malahide is just 10 minutes from the airport and easily reached. You'll find a number of outstanding Bed and Breakfast options here, including the Evergreen B&B, with especially hospitable hosts.

Castle Lodge Bed & Breakfast is another great option with spacious, comfortable rooms that will allow you to rest up and get ready for your travels throughout the Emerald Isle.

Those who stay in Malahide shouldn't miss exploring Malahide Castle, a magnificent castle with tours available that take visitors into its fascinating, historic past. For those intrigued by the paranormal, this castle is also reportedly home to at least five ghosts, including Lady Maud Plunkett, buried in the castle graveyard, and a 16th century caretaker by the name of Puck.

The Itinerary

The itinerary you'll find on the following pages is my personal favorite. Although it always seems that each time I've visited Ireland is better than the last, I think this is an ideal route for those who want to sample some of the best of Ireland without running into hordes of other tourists. While the majority of Ireland's most popular attractions are certainly well worth visiting, like the Guinness Storehouse, Glendalough, Blarney Castle and the Cliffs of Moher, this journey will take you to many destinations that few tourists venture to, yet are just as rewarding if not even more so.

I almost always begin my trip by resting up from the long journey and doing a little exploring in Dublin. We'll start there, where you'll find many interesting destinations that you probably haven't had the chance to visit, and then head out on the road.

The first stop is the Wicklow Mountains and a trek up a narrow, winding road to a B&B set in what feels like the middle of nowhere, filled with the sounds of sheep and the sights of brilliant rainbows, dazzling lakes and, of course, breathtaking mountains. Virtually no chance of a tour bus getting up here.

Next, we'll journey to the Hook Head Peninsula, a two-and-a-half-hour drive south, rarely mentioned in travel guides, yet filled with numerous attractions and scenic beauty that is sure to delight.

Portmagee, in South West Kerry is your next stop. It's a four- to five-hour trip from Hook Head, but worth the somewhat long trek. There are a number of ideal stops along the way that make for a perfect break, and when you arrive you're likely to be so in awe of the scenery, you'll completely forget how long it took you to get there.

From here, you'll travel north to Rossaveal, where you'll hop on a ferry to Inisheer Island, the smallest of the Aran Islands.

Once goodbyes are said to beautiful Inisheer, we'll explore spectacular Connemara and the town of Clifden. If you're short on time, you can return to Dublin in an easy three-hour jaunt from there with the roadways especially good between Galway and Dublin. If time allows, and you have the inclination, you may want to include an overnight at Ross Castle in County Meath. This very unique B&B is located just an hour northwest of Dublin, it's easy to get back to the city from there.

Keep in mind, this itinerary is just a guide – you might use it just as is, choose to stay overnight in other places in between, or simply use bits of the information to help you plan your own ideal trip.

Dublin

While the city of Dublin is certainly not an off the beaten path type of destination, there are many fabulous, lesser known spots that are worth visiting while you're there. You probably already know about the National Museum, St. Patrick's Cathedral and the Guinness Storehouse, but you've likely not been to some of these. Choose one, a few, or all for a more unique experience, and enjoy!

The Leprechaun Museum.

The Leprechaun Museum is right in the heart of Dublin, but somehow most just seem to pass it by without a second look. That's a shame, because while there aren't exactly leaping leprechauns greeting you around every corner, you will get to know what it feels like to be as tiny as these mischief-making little men – and, even what it's like to find that pot of gold at the end of the rainbow. This quirky, magical museum is a great way to get a humorous introduction into Irish myth and legend, including the true meaning of tales that have been told for thousands of years.

Phoenix Park

Phoenix Park is the largest city park in Europe. One of my favorite ways to get acclimated to the time difference is to take a walk or go for a run through the park and do a little people watching. There is a lot to see and do here as well, including paying a visit to the President's House which keeps a candle lit as a reminder that those who've left the country are more than welcome home. If you'd like to take a tour, be sure and call first (353-1-677-0095).

The Dublin Zoo, Ashtown Castle, and the residence of the U.S. Ambassador can all be found in Phoenix Park too.

Haunted History Tour

This tour conducted by Hidden Dublin Walking Tours features a more bewitching, eerie twist on the typical history tour. The tour guides are filled with intriguing facts that many longtime locals aren't aware of, and will reveal parts of the city that few would otherwise see on a typical vacation to Ireland. The tour provides a good balance of history, humor and spooky tales that even the most unenthusiastic teenager is sure to appreciate.

Richmond Villas Graffiti Art

Dublin is home to many amazing works of art, but not all of them can be seen in an art gallery. Instead, you'll have to head to the back alleys of Dublin, just behind The Bernard Shaw pub on Richmond Street to the Richmond Villas. Here you'll see some pretty fantastic graffiti with every wall covered with incredibly colorful images, some of which rival what you'd see in a world-class gallery.

Drimnagh Castle

Drimnagh Castle is a hidden treasure most tourists don't pencil in on their itinerary. Don't be surprised if you and your travel companions are the only visitors on any given day. This 13th century Norman castle is the only one to still retain a fully-flooded moat. It also has a massive fireplace, a formal garden, arrow slit windows and a murder hole. It's been alleged that the ghost of a young woman named Eleanora still haunts the castle and its environs. Some say she committed suicide after her husband was killed, while others say she was raped by Oliver Cromwell himself who was a frequent visitor. As a result of the trauma, she allegedly threw herself from the turrets. More than a few have even claimed to have spotted the ghost of the English ruler here as well.

Outside of Dublin proper there are a number of treasures to be discovered, like:

Howth

Howth (rhymes with both) is a picturesque fishing town just northeast of Dublin on the Howth Peninsula. It's definitely worth visiting while you're here, and if you aren't driving, you can easily take the DART (train service) from Dublin's city center at Connolly Station and be there in less than 30 minutes.

Once here, you might explore the 15th century Howth Castle, visit Baily Lighthouse and Martello Tower Museum. The museum houses an excellent collection of exhibits that chronicle the history of telecommunications from the 1840s to the present time.

This is also a wonderful area to walk with scenic paths running along the cliffs and through woodlands. In the summer, you can even take a boat trip to Ireland's Eye, an uninhabited island with ruins of an 8th century church as well as a large bird colony, including Ireland's newest gannet colony as well as puffin, great black-backed and herring gulls.

While in Howth, don't miss dining at King Sitric, which serves amazing fish 'n' chips as well as lobster 'n' chips, paired with a good pint. If the name sounds familiar, that might be because celebrity chef and author Anthony Bourdain enjoyed a meal here while filming the Travel Channel's now defunct "No Reservations" series. He's also recommended it as one of the Top 100 favorites across the globe.

Dollymount Beach and Bull Island

Dollymount Beach is just four miles (6.4 km) from Dublin's City Centre on Bull Island, often referred to by the locals as "Dollier." This beach is popular for kitesurfing, and you're likely to spot numerous kitesurfers while visiting almost any time of the year – always fun to watch. You can even drive on the beach here, it's legal and the sand is extremely compact. If you attempt it, just be sure to keep an eye on the tide so that it doesn't swallow you, or your car up, into the sea. The island is also a paradise for birdwatchers as well as a pleasant diversion from hectic city life in Dublin.

County Wicklow

After you've finished exploring Dublin, it's time to move on to County Wicklow, where your next B&B awaits less than an hour away. Some of the area's most popular visitor attractions include Powerscourt Estate and Gardens, Powerscourt Waterfall and Glendalough. If you haven't visited before, you may want to include those destinations on your must-see list as they're certainly worth visiting, just keep in mind they are hotspots for tour buses as part of the well-traveled visitor path.

On a side note, visiting Powerscourt Estate during the offseason and in-between tour buses, if you're lucky, can be a lot more rewarding. Stroll the winding paths through forests, gardens and ponds, and you may even run into a film crew. It's a frequent occurrence here and provides an interesting glimpse into the makings of a movie, provided you're visiting on a quiet day.

Lough Dan House, Roundwood

While there are numerous accommodation options throughout the county, if you want to get off the beaten path and explore places that few other tourists venture to, Lough Dan House is where you want to be. It sits more than 1,000 feet into the

Wicklow Mountains on an 80-acre farm overlooking magnificent Lough Dan, the largest natural lake in the eastern region of Ireland. Your hosts, owners Sean and Theresa Byrne are fifth-generation Byrnes, and can tell you a lot about the history of the area.

When you get to the town of Roundwood, you'll follow the signs toward Lough Dan along a narrow, winding road in order to reach Lough Dan House. Pass the sign that says "residents only," remember, you are a resident, even if just for the night, and continue on. The lake will become visible on your right, and when the road makes a sharp right turn, you'll see the house. As long as Theresa knows when you'll be arriving, she's likely to be there to direct you into the driveway, welcoming you into her home.

What to do

This is the ultimate walking/hiking destination, with so many breathtaking sights it can be difficult to choose which path to take.

Sean offers guided walks, ranging from roughly four to 12 miles, depending on your level of fitness. You'll have the opportunity to hear stories about the area as well as the people who live here.

While Sean and Theresa will be happy to point you in the right direction if you'd like to head out on your own, maps and all, I highly recommend the hike from just above Lough Tay to Lough Dan. On a beautiful, only partly cloudy late September day, I didn't see

another person on the entire seven-mile roundtrip trek. Grab one of the maps available in the greeting area for directions to Pier Gates, less than a 10-minute drive away. To park, you'll need to drive about one-quarter mile further, where you'll see a small pullout on the right. Before descending on the trail through the gate, walk directly across the road and enjoy this amazing view of Lough Tay.

Here is a glimpse of what you can expect to see on this incredibly scenic trek.

Fans of the History Channel series "Vikings," take note. This is the region used to film many shots you've seen watching this outstanding show. The steep slopes of Luggala Mountain have a Scandinavian look, while Lough Tay is the perfect location for scenes aboard the Viking longships. Does this image look familiar?

Another sight to see that few tourists get to is Glenmacnass Falls. Set between Laragh and Sally Gap, the cascade of water spills into the valley, varying from a picturesque trickle during a dry summer to a thundering torrent at times of heavy rain. To get there, follow Military Road (Route 115) towards Sally Gap. Located near the village of Laragh, you'll be just a short drive away from one of Ireland's most popular attractions, the 6th century monastic settlement of Glendalough.

Where to dine

Lough Dan House serves more than just a delicious, full Irish breakfast. You can enjoy a fine dinner here too, including beer or wine. If you'd like to try something a little different, in the town of Roundwood, Byrne & Woods Restaurant & Bar is typically filled with locals and has a cozy, non-touristy atmosphere, including dark wood and a crackling fireplace, along with some of the best food around.

Other County Wicklow sights and attractions

If you find yourself with extra time, there are a number of other interesting sights to check out, like:

Brittas Bay. One of the finest beaches on the East Coast, Brittas Bay has an over three-mile stretch of beautiful white sand dunes and clean beaches. It's been awarded an EU Blue Flag, the international emblem for the highest quality beach areas on the continent, for five consecutive years. With no headlands to interfere with its tranquil rhythm, the waters are ideal for taking a dip, enjoying a stroll across the sands or going sailing. The dunes are also home to wildlife like red fox, rabbit and badger as well as numerous plants, including several rare species.

Wicklow Gaol. This interesting, yet rather creepy, museum was opened in 1702 as a jail to hold prisoners sentenced under the repressive Penal Laws. It was notorious throughout the country for the brutality of its keepers and the harsh conditions suffered by inmates. Today, it tells the story of its prisoners through an interactive, family-friendly tour led by knowledgeable and entertaining guides. For those who aren't traveling with children, night tours for adults only will give you the chance to explore the spooky jail in the dark, mingling with the many purported ghosts.

Gardens. In addition to Powerscourt House & Gardens, there are several others worthy of a visit, including Mount Usher Gardens, particularly stunning in the fall. Kilruddy House & Gardens is an especially pleasant place to take a stroll through its 17th century garden as well as touring one of the most successful Elizabethan-Revival mansions in Ireland. The estate has made appearances in a number of well-known films and television mini-series, including "My Left Foot," "Far & Away," "Angela's Ashes," "The Tudors" and "Camelot."

Horseback riding at Glendalough House. Seeing Ireland from the back of a horse provides a unique, unforgettable experience that's sure to be one of the highlights of your time here. Glendalough House offers nearly 18 miles of rides through lush, rolling parkland and open pastures, riverside and mature oak woodlands, as well as along the top of Scar Mountain, bringing the chance to see some of the best of the spectacularly beautiful countryside.

Before you leave the area, there's a good chance you'll be thinking about making another trip to come back another time and stay longer. As Theresa told me, repeat visits to Lough Dan House for much longer stays, are becoming increasingly common, particularly for those who are looking for a nice, relaxing break without the stress of driving.

A three- to seven-day, fully-inclusive holiday package includes meeting guests at Dublin Airport – or another destination of your choosing in the city, eliminating the need to rent a car. In addition to transport to and from the airport, your accommodation, all meals, packed lunches to take along on your daily walk or other activities like horseback riding, cycling, golf and fishing, as well as transport to and from those activities, and even necessary angling gear, are all included too.

Certainly something to think about for your next trip – or, perhaps even for this one if you're so inclined.

County Wexford

Next, we'll head to County Wexford and the Hook Head Peninsula, less than a two hour's drive from County Wicklow, with a stop to visit the Dunbrody Famine Ship in New Ross.

Taking a guided tour of the ship, an authentic reproduction of the 1840s Emigrant Vessel, allows visitors to walk in the shoes of those who traveled across the Atlantic to America during the famine times. The passionate, well-informed actors bring the tales of what passengers had to endure to life.

Your final destination, for the time being anyway, is the Hook Head Peninsula, with a number of fabulous places in which to stay to suit all tastes. If you'd like to be within walking distance of great pubs and a beautiful beach, with a dining establishment just steps away from your room, the Aldridge Lodge Restaurant and Guesthouse in Duncannon village is a perfect choice. You'll enjoy superb accommodations as well as an award-winning eatery with menus featuring local and homegrown produce along with stunning views of nearby Duncannon beach, the river estuary and the Comeragh Mountains.

Roughly a five-minute drive south of Duncannon, Hook Head Bed and Breakfast is centrally located on the peninsula, in a tranquil area just a short walk from magnificent Dollar Bay and Booley Bay beaches as well as Templars Inn Bar & Restaurant. The highlight here is the especially warm welcome you'll receive from your host, Anne O'Shea. Her home is absolutely meticulous and luxuriously decorated, yet relaxed and inviting at the same time. The rooms have a real homey feel, with extremely comfy beds and windows offering picturesque views of the countryside. You can also look forward to a delicious home-cooked breakfast in the morning. Anne truly goes out of her way to ensure the utmost stay, without being overbearing, in addition to giving helpful advice about the region. During our conversations, it was obvious how excited she was to share this lovely area with visitors, noting that it's one of the rare places in Ireland that isn't filled with touristy shops – some Irish refer to them as "Hi-Diddly-Dee" shops – selling the same Made In China trinkets you see everywhere else.

What to do

You'll have a long list of things to choose from on the Hook Head Peninsula when it comes to what to see or do.

Hook Lighthouse. The oldest working lighthouse in the world, this structure as it stands today has existed for 800 years, though monks reportedly lit a beacon here as long ago as the 5th century. In the mid-17th century, the monks were replaced by the first lighthouse keepers, and in 1996, it was converted to automatic operation. Take a guided tour, available through the adjacent visitor center. Climbing the 115 steps to the balcony brings especially dramatic vistas on a clear day.

Tintern Abbey. The abbey, situated on the west shores of Bannow Bay, was one of the most powerful Cistercian foundations in the region until the Dissolution of the Monasteries in 1536. It was built around the turn of the 13th century by William Marshal, Earl of Pembroke, who set sail for Ireland on his first visit as Lord of Leinster. His ship was damaged by a storm and threatened to wreck during the voyage. William vowed that if he and the crew survived, he would build a church wherever he landed. Upon reaching safety in Bannow Bay, he redeemed his vow, bequeathing about 9,000 acres of land for the abbey.

Though Tintern Abbey is only open to visitors during the summer, the grounds are open all year, and seeing the exterior is really the highlight anyway. From here, you can take a walk along the river, crossed by two bridges, to explore an old church and graveyard. Avid walkers might want to take the longer route from the village of Saltmills nearby. To do so, drive east through the village on L4043, pass the one small shop and take the next left at the sign for Vine Cottage Bar & Beer Garden. Park near the bar and then continue down the road on foot. The road gradually becomes a dirt trail, following the river all the way to the abbey.

Colclough Walled Garden. This lovingly restored 2.5-acre walled garden was built by the Colclough Family in the early 19th century. It can be reached via the wooded trails near Tintern Abbey. Restoration work began in 2010, with the layout of the garden reinstated to what it was back in 1838.

Loftus Hall. This rather ominous looking mansion is a unique tourist attraction. From the moment you drive up to its

gates and down the long driveway to where it sits on a section of rather desolate landscape, you're likely to sense something strange has happened here. Take a tour, and don't forget to bring your ghost hunting gear if you want to explore what's claimed to be Ireland's most haunted house.

Duncannon Fort. Duncannon Fort dates from 1588, when it was built to repel the Spanish Armada and to prevent pirates from plundering merchant ships of their riches as they made their way up the harbor. The fort was last used and rebuilt by the Irish Army during World War II. Today, it houses an art gallery, a toy museum, maritime and military museum, officers' tea room and a craft shop. Guided tours are available on the hour Sunday through Friday.

The beaches. There are 14 beaches that can be found on the Hook Peninsula, with all types of water activities available in the summer, such as kite surfing, surfing, body boarding and kayaking. Duncannon beach is a one-mile long stretch of sand that plays host to the sand castle building festival held in August each year. When the weather is right, Hooked Kite Surfing provides kite surfing and stand up paddleboarding lessons here too.

If you're looking for a more secluded beach, you can't go wrong with Dollar Bay and Booley Bay beaches, situated next to each other just off Hook Head Road. The bay is sheltered, providing a great spot to swim or to just relax on the soft, clean sand.

Where to eat

Templars Inn. If you're staying at Hook Head B&B, Templars Inn is just a short walk from there. The restaurant serves up fresh seafood, including locally-caught crab claws, along with a number of options for non-seafood eaters, like chicken, steak and lamb.

The Strand Tavern. Located in the heart of Duncannon, The Strand Tavern may not look like much on the outside, but here you'll find what may be one of your favorite meals in Ireland. This seaside tavern features a varied menu with fresh seafood, including steamed mussels and creamy seafood chowder as well as lamb, beef and chicken dishes.

Aldridge Lodge Restaurant. The Aldridge Lodge is yet another outstanding choice when you're looking for the very best. It's the holder of the prestigious Michelin Bib Gourmand and has also won a number of Food and Wine magazine awards. Dine on local, homegrown produce and an ever-changing menu featuring items like Grilled Hook Head Lobster, beef, venison and lamb.

County Wexford to County Kerry: What to See Along the Way

As the next stop on the itinerary, Portmagee, is a four- to five-hour drive west, you may want to break up the journey into two days, spending the night along the way, or enjoying quick breaks here and there depending on the amount of time you have. As Portmagee is one of my favorite towns in all of Ireland, I usually just want to get there as quickly as possible.

There are a multitude of options, but don't rely on Google Maps to get you there. The fastest route is the E30 from New Ross through the city of Waterford and further west to Dungarvan. Just before the town of Dungarvan, you'll take the N72 toward Fermoy, and eventually past Killarney to the N70, bringing you out to the coast and close to Portmagee.

A few highlights along this route include:

Dungarvan Castle. This castle is in the process of being renovated in stages. It consists of a polygonal shell keep with an enclosing curtain wall, corner tower and a gate tower. The shell keep dates from the 12th century. The barracks have been restored and currently house an informative exhibition about the history of the castle. Admission is free.

Lismore Castle. The magnificent castle itself, which dates back to 1170, cannot be toured, though it is available to rent for those who have the means. The beautiful surrounding gardens

can be toured, or you can always just make a quick stop to take a picture of the castle from the Blackwater River Bridge.

If you've not explored Killarney National Park, you might want to follow the N71 south once you reach Killarney. This route is narrow and winding in spots, but also incredibly scenic as you'll travel through breathtaking mountains, eventually descending down to Kenmare Bay and the Atlantic coast. Allow lots of extra time, as you'll not only be forced to drive slowly due to the roads, but there are many picture-postcard spots along the way, and you won't want to miss the opportunity.

County Kerry

As you drive into Portmagee, you might just feel as if you're "coming home." At least that's what many other travelers before you, and me, have described. You're likely to already be on a natural "high" having experienced some of the most scenic areas in all of Ireland – and that's saying a lot in a country that's filled with spectacular views in all directions.

This charming seaside fishing village features a row of brightly colored buildings that seem to add a cheery feel, even on a dreary day. You'll also find a rich and colorful history along with especially friendly locals.

There are a number of excellent accommodation options, but I've found that staying at The Moorings is not only the most convenient, as it's set adjacent to The Bridge Bar with its frequent traditional music nights, ever-flowing Guinness and incredible cuisine, but it also has super comfy beds. The Superior Seaview rooms overlook the village harbor and can be rented at very reasonable rates, including excellent Wi-Fi and a delicious breakfast with a variety of menu options.

For those on a tight budget, a very nice ensuite room (with private bathroom) can be had at the local hostel, Skellig Ring House, starting as low as 19.50 to 23€ per night, depending on the season and day of the week. Rooms with shared bathrooms start at 15 to 20€ per night. It's just a short walk to town from here.

Portmagee Heights is another good choice if you're looking for a traditional B&B, offering unobstructed views overlooking the village, harbor and Valentia Island. It's about a five-minute walk into town from there.

Carraig Liath House on Valentia Island has spacious rooms, a delicious breakfast and beautiful views overlooking Portmagee. It's just a short stroll across the bridge to the village.

What to do

Although this magical village is quite small, you'll find many different things to do throughout the area.

Kerry Cliffs. This family-run attraction is located just outside of town. Some may question having to pay to see the cliffs, but admission is just 4€ (about $5) and is one of the best spots from which to see some of the most breathtaking cliffs in the region, along with the Skellig Rocks. They're also said to be the closest viewing point to the rocky isles once known as the Skel-locks, in addition to being near Puffin Island, the home of some 10,000 Atlantic puffins. The site also features a small gift shop and coffee shop with indoor and outdoor seating – a wonderful place to enjoy a hot beverage after what's often a rather chilly walk, particularly at the cliffs

where it can get quite windy. In my opinion, it is worth the effort and small fee for the reward of such fantastic views.

Skelligs Chocolate Factory. This small, family-run chocolate factory sits along the Ring of Kerry at the edge of St. Finian's Bay, roughly five-and-a-half-miles (9 kilometers) from Portmagee. While it's fun to visit anytime, it makes for a perfect spot to duck into on a rainy day. You can watch the chocolate being made, enjoy samples and take some back home too. There are boxes in various sizes that are perfect for a gift, or for yourself to indulge in during your travels. The Irish Whiskey Creme Truffles are absolutely amazing, but really, so is everything else.

A coffee shop serving tea, coffee, the factory's own delicious hot chocolate as well as fresh, homemade cakes and other desserts is onsite too.

Coastal walk. There are numerous scenic walks available, but the Bolus Loop Walk is one that's really not to be missed. If you continue on the Ring of Kerry just past the chocolate factory, you'll see a narrow road to your right that follows the coast. There's just room enough for one vehicle at a time so you'll need to drive slowly and use turnouts as necessary, but with some of the best views in all of Ireland, who wants to drive fast? It will lead you to the Bolus Loop Walk trailhead, a 5.6-mile trek (9 km), which begins at the small car park at the monument to the American Liberator, which crashed off the Skelligs back in 1944. It's a moderately easy walk, mostly along high cliffs, passing countless sheep with panoramic vistas of the Atlantic and Skellig Rocks.

Portmagee Heritage Trail. Follow this short trail that begins at St. Patrick's Church, to learn more about the village. It features a number of plaques as well as points of interest where you'll find out how Portmagee got its name, learn about the history of the church and the "Old Year" celebration, the story of Lovers Lane, wild birds in the area and more.

Boat trip to the Skelligs. The Skellig Islands are situated about eight miles off the coast of Portmagee. These majestic "rocks" impressively rise up out of the sea, with the largest, a UNESCO heritage site since 1996, Skellig Michael (AKA Great Skellig) soaring into the clouds at 714 feet above sea level. Often enshrouded in mist, atop its summit lies an incredibly well-preserved 6th century monastic settlement. If you can get there, it's likely to be the highlight of your time in Ireland.

Boat trips are available for viewing the natural monuments up close, generally running from late April to late September, if the weather cooperates. The seas here can be treacherous, which means trips are often cancelled so you'll have to hope for a calm day to enjoy the rewards of climbing up and down the historic 600 steps of this Early Christian site. The boat trip takes about 45 minutes, and you'll have two- to two-and-a-half hours up on the rock. The boat will also stop at Little Skellig providing a chance to view the second largest gannet colony in the world – some 23,000 pairs nest on every available ledge.

The Skellig Experience. The Skellig Experience is a visitor center/ museum which tells the story of the Skellig Rocks. If you're not able to make the boat trip, you can come here to find out about the monks who lived on the desolate rocks as well as the marine life and seabirds in the area. Exhibits reveal the history and archaeology of the monastery, the seabirds, lighthouses and the underwater world. A short documentary, "Island On the Edge of the World," is also featured in the center's auditorium.

Valentia Island. Linked to Portmagee via a bridge, the island is packed with incredible natural beauty, with its western region dominated by the barren, dramatic cliffs of Bray Head, providing jaw-dropping views of the coastline as well as lush and colorful vegetation.

If you're up for a great walk, the Bray Head Loop is a 4.3-mile route along the coast at the west end of the island with a steady climb up to Bray Tower at the summit. From here you'll enjoy fabulous views of the Atlantic, The Skelligs, Portmagee and Puffin Island. If sudden bad weather comes in, the roof of the structure is intact, providing a perfect shelter for ducking out of the elements. Near the car park is the historic site where the first Trans-Atlantic cable landed in1866, connecting North America to the rest of the world. At the time, Valentia Island was considered the center of the world for communications.

Be sure to look out for the sign that will direct you to the Tetrapod Trackway. The Tetrapod footprints are said to be the most extensive of the four Devonian trackways on earth. The others are located in Genoa River and Glen Isla, Australia and Tarbet Ness, Scotland. The imprints are believed to be somewhere between 350 and 370 million years old and represent the transition of life from water to land, a significant turning point in evolution as well as being the oldest reliably dated evidence of amphibians moving over land.

From the Geokaun Mountain and Fogher Cliffs, you can take in awe-inspiring 360-degree views, including Dingle, The Blaskets, the mountains of Kerry and the Atlantic, extending as far west as the eye can see. It's a steep climb, but certainly worth the effort – and, if you aren't up for that much of a workout, you can drive, or park at one of the three areas at various intervals on the way up, making it accessible and enjoyable for all. There is an entrance fee of 5€ per car or 2€ per pedestrian.

Follow the road down to the Cromwell Point Lighthouse for even more impressive views. It's also open for tours from May through September.

The surrounding waters are also renowned for diving, featured in National Geographic as well as other publications. There are multiple dive sites across the island, including at Bray Head, Valentia Harbour, Knightstown Pier and Doulous Head. If you're interested, contact Valentia Island Sea Sports & Adventures in Knightstown for more information.

The center of action on the island is Knightstown, though it can be pretty quiet here during the offseason. Enjoy a short stroll by taking the Altazamuth Walk, beginning at the Altazamuth Stone on Jane Street leading down to the seafront, edged by wildlife habitats and brilliant gardens. The small town also boasts an outstanding pub, Boston's Bar & Restaurant, with high quality meals and a friendly atmosphere, as well as being a great place to warm up with an Irish coffee.

Where to eat. After all that walking and sight-seeing, you're bound to have worked up an appetite. You can't go wrong by enjoying a meal at The Moorings Restaurant or high-end pub grub at The Bridge Bar next door. Not only is it conveniently right downstairs from the rooms at The Moorings, you'll be able to enjoy award-winning cuisine that typically features a bounty of fresh seafood, Irish beef, local produce and homemade brown bread.

Favorites at the bar include the Guinness beef stew, seafood chowder and fresh Portmagee crab claws. The Moorings offers many delights, including vegetarian fare, the fresh catch of the day, steak, chicken and my favorite, pan-fried fillet of Hake, Atlantic prawn & spring onion mash. With so many different options available between the bar and the restaurant, there's really no need, and you'll probably have no desire, to venture anywhere else.

After dinner, stick around awhile and enjoy traditional Irish music and set dance on Friday and Sunday nights. In July and August, Tuesday night is Irish night, where you can listen, dance and sing along to great local musicians. There are numerous events held here throughout the year, bringing out talent from near and far, including the annual Sea Shanty Festival, when the bar is filled with lots of cheer and song, from singers, musicians and patrons alike.

Getting to Inisheer Island

You'll need to take a ferry to get to Inisheer Island, and while there are a few different options, it's best to take the Rossaveal, County Galway ferry rather than hop aboard in Doolin. When the sea gets rough, the Doolin ferries out to the Aran Islands are often cancelled, while Rossaveal ferries are almost always able to get you there. While getting stuck in Doolin wouldn't be the worst thing in the world, if you don't visit Inisheer Island, you'll be missing out on what may be a once in a lifetime experience. Thanks to the advice of my wonderful host Maria at South Aran House, I managed to avoid what would have been a huge disappointment.

Driving directly from Portmagee to Rossaveal takes a little over four hours. The charming town of Adare, while certainly not a "less traveled destination" and a bit touristy, makes a perfect spot for a break at about the midpoint of your journey.

Adare is a beautiful village filled with thatched cottages, several ancient churches and two castles, one of which serves as the luxury Adare Manor Hotel. The 13th century Desmond Castle, located at the edge of the village, can be toured between June and September.

If you're looking for an upscale lunch, you can't go wrong with The Blue Door, set in a romantic thatched cottage that dates back to the early 1830s. It's situated right along Main Street so you can't miss it. While prices aren't exorbitant, they are a little steep, so be prepared if you're on a budget.

The Dovecot Restaurant is a more low-key, affordable spot inside the Adare Heritage Center, serving up tasty food and reasonable prices, with especially delicious cakes. While you're here, you can also do a little souvenir shopping or view the historical exhibition that includes a reconstruction of the town's past from the arrival of the Normans in the 12th century to the ancient abbeys of the Middle Ages.

Back on the road again, it's just a half hour's drive northwest to Bunratty Castle in Shannon, a popular attraction right along the way. While it's definitely touristy, it's still fun to visit, providing a fascinating journey through Irish history. The 13th century castle offers self-guided tours, with highlights including a dungeon. During medieval times, prisoners were blinded and told to walk 13 steps – unfortunately for them, there were only 12, which meant when the prisoner took that 13th step he would fall to the bottom, a more than 10-foot drop into total darkness.

The medieval furniture and art collection is simply stunning. Highlights include a 16th century Armada table, a 15th century painting of St. Peter and the Apostles, an elaborately carved 16th century oak bed and several 16th century tapestries.

From Shannon, you're about an hour and 40 minutes from Rossaveal, though Galway can get a bit congested so you might want to allow a little extra time to ensure you'll make your scheduled ferry.

Ferry reservations can, and should, be made in advance online. Aran Island Ferries provides reliable, year-round service and it takes a little less than an hour to get to the island. You can leave your vehicle at the Ferry Car Park located just before the pier in Rossaveal near the T-junction. The attendant will direct you to the correct ferry. The current rate is 5€ per day, due upon your return.

Enjoy the ride, and perhaps some great conversation about what to expect on the island with friendly ferry engineer Adrian Van Steen, a Dutch transplant – and, if you remember, tell him I said hello. Before you know it, you'll be whisked away to what feels like a whole new world.

Inisheer Island

Inisheer, technically known as Inis Oírr, is the smallest of the three Aran Islands, bringing the chance to experience Old World Ireland, with Irish being the main language for islanders. At just two-square-miles, the island is also extremely walkable, though you will find some options for transportation, including hiring a traditional "Pony & Trap" at the pier upon arrival. Or, you can just stop one as it clip-clops around the island's maze of paths. It's a great way to see the island and learn about island life from friendly, local drivers.

Bicycling is also a good way to get around, with bikes of all sizes available for rent right at the top of the pier.

If you've reserved your accommodations in advance – and you should if you haven't already – your B&B host may be able to pick you up right at the pier when you arrive, allowing you to get a night's rest before deciding how you'd like to explore the island.

Speaking of accommodations, Enda and Maria Conneely, the fabulous hosts at South Aran House, offer incredible hospitality and a very comfortable stay in a home with heated floors and spectacular water views. Guests also enjoy delicious breakfasts (included in the very reasonable rates of 39€ per person or 49€ single occupancy) and dinners at their own eatery just a short walk down the road, Fisherman's Cottage Restaurant. Guests can also book a variety of retreats and lifestyle courses here, such as cookery, yoga and Pilates.

Hostel accommodations are available at Brú Radharc Na Mara, a family-run hostel open between March and October. Located near the ferry port, pubs, shops and the beach, you'll find four- to six-bed dorms, family rooms and private rooms.

What to do

Inisheer is ideal for those who are looking for a quiet retreat to contemplate life or to enjoy creative pursuits like writing or painting, with numerous inspiring landscapes. Those who want to get out and explore will find lots to do as well.

As the island is so small, walking its perimeter makes for an ideal eight-mile trek that will allow you to get up close and personal with many of its delights. Or, just get lost on the paths that wind

through stone walls, discovering heritage sites, holy wells, sculptures, rare plants and birds.

Visitors can go snorkeling or diving in the clear waters that surround the island, viewing remains of old wrecks near Finnis Rock along with an abundance of marine life. On the island's north end, you'll find beautiful sandy beaches for soaking in the sun and swimming in the summer.

On the eastern shore, enjoy picturesque views of

the Cliffs of Moher, a lighthouse and a shipwreck. The cargo vessel, "Plassey," was wrecked here in the 1960s. Islanders rescued the entire crew during a vicious storm and were able to save each and every sailor. Over time, the waves have thrown the wreck upon the rocks, well above the high tide mark.

Fans of the 1990s Irish television series, "Father Ted," will recognize the wreck from the show's opening credits.

Other sights include:

Tobar Éanna. The holy well of St. Enda, patron saint of the Aran Islands. This revered well is said to have healing powers. The islanders say it never runs dry, and if you walk around it seven times, praying the rosary as you do, look inside it and see an eel in the water, you'll be healed of all that ails you. But, it only works if you actually see the eel.

On your way out to the well, you'll pass an incredible sculpture set above the water, a memorial to honor islanders lost at sea, created by fine arts sculptor Alexandra Morosco. The stone depicts a curragh caught in a wave and is inscribed with words by poet laureate Martin O'Direan:

"Maireann a gcuimhne fós i m'aigne

Is mairfidh cinnte go dté mé i dtalamh."

"Their memory is in my mind still

And will surely remain till I go into the clay."

Teampall Chaomhán. This medieval church ruin half buried in the sand in the island graveyard is home to another legend: If you can squeeze through the very narrow, tall window at the front of the church, going from the outside in, stepping onto the stone altar, you're said to be guaranteed to go to heaven when your time has come.

Caisleán Uí Bhríain. An imposing three-story 16th century tower house built by the O'Brien family within a Stone Age fort.

Cnoc Raithni. An ancient burial mound dating back to the Bronze Age, evidence of the earliest settlers to the island.

Where to eat

Fisherman's Cottage Restaurant, in my opinion, has the best meals on the island, but only breakfast and dinner is served, and you're bound to get hungry in between, especially if you do a lot of walking.

Nigh Ted, just down the road, serves a great lunch with to-die-for seafood chowder along with a warm welcome and beautiful views. If you're lucky, you might even get to see dolphins swimming in the bay.

Another option if you're just looking for some food for a picnic or while you're walking around the island, is to go to the local grocery shop located adjacent to Tigh Ruairi (Rory's) B&B and pick up some goodies to take along with you.

County Galway and Connemara

After making your return to the mainland in County Galway, it's time to explore beautiful Connemara. This breathtaking, unspoiled region is home to the Twelve Bens Mountain Range along with picture-perfect golden beaches, charming towns and stunning castles.

Clifden, set along the coast of Connemara, is less than an hour's drive from Rossaveal, and an ideal town to stay while exploring the region's abbeys, castle ruins, national parks, mountains and beaches. You'll also find lots of fun local shops, with everything from antiques to wool sweaters and gifts. Clifden is becoming increasingly popular for its food scene, with a number of fine eateries as well as lively pubs featuring music all year round.

If you want to splurge on a luxury stay at some point during your trip, now may be the perfect time. Clifden is the home of Abbeyglen Castle Hotel, one of my favorite places to stay in all of Ireland. I was lucky, back in 2001, when all flights on Aer Lingus were cancelled due to a strike on the very day I was supposed to fly home. With an extra five days in the country, I made my way to Connemara and discovered this magnificent hotel while wandering the back roads. Since then, I've returned several times and have never been disappointed. Ask for a superior room or luxury suite with a four-poster bed and fireplace if you really want a stay to remember.

The hotel also provides award-winning gourmet cuisine in its on-site restaurant, including fresh seafood, live lobster and Connemara lamb along with frequent live music.

If you'd prefer an inexpensive but comfortable accommodation option, there are a number of other good choices in the area, including:

Clifden Town Hostel, located in the center of town, with double, triple, quad and five-bed rooms, with singles available in the off-season. Rates start at just 21€ a night and include the use of two self-catering kitchens and Wi-Fi.

Ben View House is a family-owned B&B, in business since 1926, offering comfortable in-town accommodations starting at 35€ per person for a double and 45€ for singles.

Atlantic View B&B is nestled between the Sky Road Peninsula and Streamstown Bay, featuring beautiful water views and rates as low as 35€ per person for a double.

What to do

While Clifden and Connemara are certainly not lesser known destinations, there are many hidden gems to be discovered in the region along with popular attractions.

The Quiet Man Bridge. If you've seen the 1952 classic film starring John Wayne and Maureen O'Hara, "The Quiet Man," you won't want to miss viewing the picturesque bridge which marks one of the most poignant scenes in the movie. It arches over a rushing stretch of the

Owenriff River, five miles (8 km) past Oughterard heading west on the N59.

Dan O'Hara's Homestead. This museum site features the home of Dan from Connemara of the renowned ballad, "Dan O'Hara," as well as an interactive farm museum and reconstructions of a ring fort, clochan (dry-stone hut), turf cutting demonstrations and jaunting car rides. The farm is also home to the world famous Connemara ponies as well as cattle, sheep, chicken and a few friendly donkeys.

Ballyconneely. It's worth making the 20 minute drive to Ballyconneely for the smoked fish available at Connemara Smokehouse alone (located atop Bunowen Pier), but you'll find a wealth of other things to do here, including viewing some of the most unspoiled landscapes in the region. Ballyconneely is renowned for its breeding of the Connemara pony – and, visiting the area brings the unique opportunity to explore it on horseback. The Point Pony Trekking & Horse Riding Centre sits next to the edge of the Atlantic, offering rides along spectacular beaches and the open countryside with the Twelve Bens as the backdrop, suitable for all levels of riders.

While you're here, don't miss the Coral Strand at Derrygimla, known for its fine coral sands. In the summer, this is also a great spot to take a dip in the water as it tends to be just a bit warmer than other beaches. There are also a number of tide pools for exploring.

Hiking. Connemara is known for some of the best hikes in all of Ireland. While Connemara National Park is home to several outstanding treks, like the Diamond Hill Loop, it also tends to be rather crowded. If you'd like to avoid bumping elbows with others out on the trail there are many other options, including Mount

Errisbeg. This fairly small mountain stands at 977 feet and can be accessed about three miles (5 km) south of Roundstone on the R341. You'll see a gate off a bend in the road that can be climbed, with a path ascending to the summit on the right. It takes less than an hour to get to the top, where you'll see the Connemara coast, the Aran Islands, Roundstone, Clifden and the Twelve Bens.

By climbing the highest of the Bens, the nearly 2,400-feet Benbaun, you'll enjoy views of Croagh Patrick and Clew Bay to the north and the Aran Islands to the south. It can be accessed from Glencorbet Valley off the R344. There is no trail per se, but navigation is easy, provided it's a clear day and the summit is visible.

There are many other hikes/walks throughout the region. If you plan to spend a lot of time hiking while you're here, Walk Connemara (www.walkconnemara.com) provides more detailed information and an extensive list of options.

If you're not up for a long walk or the weather isn't cooperating, you might want to take a drive down Sky Road, with its numerous points for fabulous pictures. In the town of Clifden itself you'll find lots of interesting shops to browse and pubs to pop in for a pint, often featuring great live music too. Among the dozens of shops, you'll find antiques, Irish knitwear and woolens, boutique designer stores, artisan wares, fashion and more.

A few of the more well-known attractions in the area include:

Connemara National Park, featuring a visitor center, scenic mountains, woodlands, bogs and grasslands.

Kylemore Abbey & Victorian Walled Garden which includes a magnificent 19th century castle, Neo-Gothic church, pottery studio, craft shop, woodland walks and a restaurant.

Roundstone Village, a popular holiday resort destination with a traditional craft center offers a number of activities including Connemara instrument making, pottery and jewelry making. A busy harbor also awaits, with local fishermen preparing and returning with the day's catch which typically includes a mix of crab, shrimp, cod, lobster, mackerel and more.

Celtic Crystal. Located in the village of Moycullen, about an hour's drive east of Clifden and 15 minutes before Galway City, this fine crystal producer is well worth a stop on the drive back to Dublin. It's a family-run business featuring special, limited edition and one-of-a-kind pieces. It tends to be more affordable and as beautiful, if not more so, than the more famous Waterford Crystal down south. Factory tours are available and include a live glass cutting demonstration.

Where to eat and play after dark

Walsh's Bakery is a wonderful spot to stop for coffee or tea along with fresh-baked desserts. You'll also find handcrafted sandwiches made with just-out-of-the-oven breads, perfect for taking along on a picnic.

Mitchell's Seafood Restaurant is a local favorite with a cozy ambiance and open fires on both its floors. The menu features locally-sourced fish as well as a wide range of other meat and vegetarian dishes. Unfortunately, if you're visiting in November, December or January, you'll be out of luck as it's closed during this period.

Guys Bar & Snug is another excellent option with delicious cuisine at affordable prices, including bangers and mash, fish 'n' chips, mussels and hot soups – wonderful on a rainy day. Stick around and enjoy great live music too.

Mannion's Bar is a fun pub where you can enjoy live music sessions and a bowl of tasty seafood chowder.

Lowry's Bar may look like a cramped, hole-in-the-wall kind of joint, but it's a great place to hang out for a while. The oldest continuously family-owned pub and in the same family since 1949, here you'll find some 120 different whiskeys to choose from along with traditional music sessions seven nights a week, from March 17 to November 1 every year.

If you're staying at Abbeyglen, the cuisine and service are exceptional, as mentioned, with a menu that includes local seafood, live lobster and Connemara lamb. Don't miss Irish night if you're here on a Tuesday, featuring traditional Irish fare and wonderful music to go along with it.

Ross Castle, County Meath

As mentioned at the beginning of the book, if you have extra time and the inclination, you may want to enjoy a "grand finale" by staying at Ross Castle in County Meath. A three-hour drive from Clifden, the castle is located in the town of Oldcastle, just an hour away from Dublin.

Ross Castle isn't anything like those five-star luxury properties, such as Ashford or Drumoland. Or, even Abbeyglen, with its more laid-back elegance. The good news, it makes a castle stay a lot more affordable, and it definitely feels like the real deal when it comes to medieval castles, along with a very unique, unforgettable experience. If you're a clean freak, you may want to pass. Construction began on the castle in 1533, nearly 500 years ago. The tower was completed in 1537, while the great hall and further extensions were finished in 1539. While stunning in its own way with lots of character, the castle is not absent of dust and spider webs.

Caretakers Sam and Benita are very welcoming – in fact, you may feel as if you're visiting family, rather than staying in a stranger's home. I spent the evening watching television, chatting with Sam and their two kids in the family room before heading up to bed for the night. Staying in a tower room is really a must for an authentic medieval castle stay, but you will need to climb up quite a few steep, winding stairs to get there. Keep in mind that bringing oversized luggage isn't a good idea unless you want a serious workout.

As the castle is somewhat isolated, Benita serves up delicious two-course and four-course dinners at 20 € and 30 € respectively, including vegetarian options, so there is really no need to leave in order to enjoy a great meal. You can also use the kitchen to cook your own, or even call for Chinese food delivery.

Do be aware that some refer to Ross Castle as a ghost hunter's paradise, with quite a few recounting tales of the paranormal during their stay, though certainly nothing harmful. You can read the stories of the purported ghosts of Richard Nugent AKA Black Baron, Myles Slasher O'Reilly as well as young lovers Sabena and Orwen, here. Lonely Planet lists Ross Castle as one of the "Ten Lesser Known Haunted Places in the World."

During my night in the castle, the heavy door of my tower room did somehow open up on its own. Whether a spirit or some type of other energy is responsible is anyone's guess. Sam and Benita's teenage son had a more harrowing night. The family doesn't usually stay in the castle, but at the time, their farmhouse down the road was being remodeled. In the morning at breakfast, he looked visibly disturbed, explaining that he felt a presence next to him on the bed as he tried to sleep, failing miserably with the thought of "something" right there.

There is no doubt that the castle has an eerie feel to it. If those walls could talk I'm sure they would tell some extremely fascinating stories.

While the castle is the main attraction, there are several other sites to see in the area while you're here, including:

Loughcrew Cairns, a series of approximately 30 tombs set across a ridge of four hills just outside the town of Oldcastle. The tombs are similar in age to the monuments in Dowth, Knowth and Newgrange – c. 3000 BC. Located on the highest point in the county, you'll enjoy beautiful views of the surrounding landscape from the cairns. If you arrive between October and May, just pick up a key to Cairn T from the coffee shop at Loughcrew Gardens.

Castlekieran, a monastic site located between Oldcastle and Kells, is an interesting site featuring a desolate church with a graveyard covered by tall grass, an Ogham stone and Kieran's Well. Sir William Wilde, father of the famous Irish writer and poet, described it as one of the most beautiful holy wells in Ireland. Tradition suggests the water has curative powers, particularly for toothaches and headaches.

A Final Note

It's hard not to have a wonderful time visiting Ireland, but the best way to ensure you enjoy a fantastic holiday is to go with an adventurous attitude, and remember that things aren't always the same in other places like they are at home – especially when traveling overseas.

While Irish people tend to be some of the friendliest, most welcoming on earth, please don't ask questions like "Where do the leprechauns live?" Or, "Why aren't there more redheads?" Seriously, tourists ask questions like these all the time.

A few other don'ts:

Never forget the basic rule of driving on the left. Every year tourists get into accidents because they're driving on the wrong side of the road.

Don't compare everything to what it's like back home – or, expect everything to be the same, such as the same brands, restaurants and other national chains. It just makes you sound like you'd rather be back home. The differences are what makes traveling fun!

Don't expect your server at a restaurant to immediately bring you the check when you're finished eating. The Irish take a relaxed view when it comes to settling the bill – and, they might look at you a little funny if you refer to it as a check for obvious reasons. Often times, when your server thinks all guests at a table are finished, he or she will leave the bill with the cashier. You'll just need to get up and settle it there. If you aren't sure, or need to leave quickly, just ask. Whatever you do, don't be rude and get upset because the bill wasn't left on your table, something I've seen several times. It's actually considered respectful not to leave it, allowing patrons to exit at their leisure, enjoying conversation after a meal without feeling rushed.

Finally, to discover the "real Ireland," don't rush. Take your time and savor each and every moment.

If you have any questions or comments in regard to planning your upcoming trip, or about this book, I would love to help. Please feel free to email me at kcdermody@gmail.com.

Look for my next book in this series including a new itinerary featuring lesser known destinations in 2016.

Until then –

Sláinte!

33945647R00035

Made in the USA
Middletown, DE
20 January 2019